To:
Love,

Our Love Story is Beautiful

Coloring Card

Sandy Mahony
Mary Lou Brown

one
love
one
heart

Hugs and Kisses

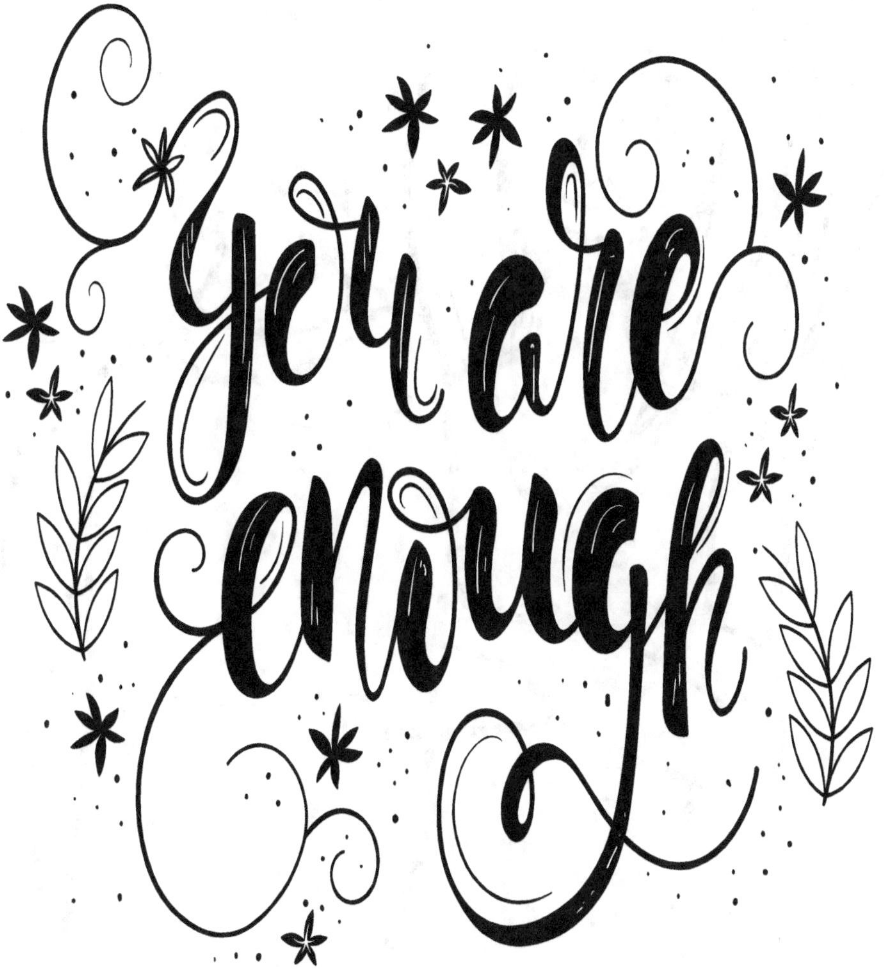
You are
enough

I love being yours

Be
MY
VALENTINE
FOR THE
Rest of my
LIFE
I Love You.

you
make me
happy

You're
my
favorite

Every love story is beautiful

fall in love with me

YOU WILL

forever

BE MY

always

I love
you
to
The Moon
AND BACK

love changes everything

adventurelearningpress.com

www.ingramcontent.com/pod-product-compliance
Lightning Source LLC
Chambersburg PA
CBHW072016280526
45788CB00005B/2069